UNNAMED CANYON

UNNAMED CANYON

poems by
BRIAN GLASER

SHANTI ARTS PUBLISHING

BRUNSWICK, MAINE

Published by Shanti Arts Publishing

Interior and cover design by Shanti Arts Designs

Shanti Arts LLC
193 Hillside Road
Brunswick, Maine 04011
shantiarts.com

Cover image by Mason Field / unsplash.com

Printed in the United States of America

ISBN: 978-1-962082-44-0 (softcover)

Library of Congress Control Number: 2024948592

CONTENTS

THE TEACHER

MORE

"Clarity and stillness are the rectification of the world."

—*Daode Jing*, translated by Louis Komjathy

THE TEACHER

m

LUNAR LIGHT

1

On the surface
I am a symptom of an insane society.

I believed the Illuminati
were conspiring to kill and eat
my firstborn,

only sane enough to know
how most would see me.

And yet the intelligence services
of various nations,
including my own,
probably do make me an object of surveillance.

To a fault, I embrace
clarity, transparency—

how to talk about the Uvalde shooting
with my sons?

2

It may be unnecessary, that conversation.

We talked about the shooting matter-of-factly,
disparaged the politicians,
moved on at dinner to other subjects.

In this way I thought I was fine
after the brother of a high school classmate
was assassinated in his kitchen.

He came home,
a latch-key kid,—
at the time I thought I was untouched.

There was a rumor it was retribution
against the father.

Now, thirty years later,
when I am insane I brood on this killing,
wondering whom I have wronged,
certain I have wronged someone.

8

The essence of being damned
is powerlessness.

I do not love power—
my fear of powerlessness does not take that form.

Nor can I believe in a God
who punishes sinners with eternal damnation.

I think of my faithful niece who judges me
for getting married in a Catholic church
and not raising Catholic children.

When my son was six or seven, the three of us
walked together in the graveyard
of the Santa Barbara mission.

Where did they go, the dead,
if they are not here?
my son asked.

It's a mystery,
I replied.

How could one condemn that response?
Who could hate me
for what I don't know?

12

A friend from Nicaragua says she doesn't believe
the outpouring of grief and resolve
following the Uvalde shooting.

Justice for brown people is still
as unreal as a dream.

My paranoia is rooted in
fear for the safety of my children.

What does it have to tell me?

That I understand the world as cruelly conspiring
to harm young people.

My worst nightmare is that I am complicit in this.

The coldness of my Kleinian analyst—
in that coldness I learned that I could no longer be a child.

But where had gone the child that I was?
Who had taken him?

14

Lacan says to embrace your symptoms.
When I am paranoid,
they pursue me like a fire.
I cannot embrace them.

But when I am sane—
then what is my disability?

I think it is a heightened sense of our vulnerability—
everyone's—
and especially children's.

Sane I can embrace my symptoms
more like a bloody boxer,
face swollen,
hugging his opponent to preempt a blow,
leaning in,
oblivious to how he is seen by those outside the ring.

THESIS

Remembering tonight the emergency room
where I waited with my mother
for admission to the psych ward
after she had threatened me with a knife—

we waited for hours,
long enough to overhear two male nurses
talk about the hopeless brain injury
of a man admitted with a gunshot wound
that evening from Santa Ana,

long enough to overhear a female nurse
ask a strung out young woman
if she knew the father of the baby she was carrying,
and to overhear the young woman say no—

A story about the body:
we all have one,

a body, that is—

the story of our body some of us never learn,
though I posit it as true
we've all made someone afraid.

DARKNESS AND LIGHT

I wondered for years why, if the pull of a black hole
is so strong,
why is it not the fate of everything
to be drawn and crushed inside of it.

Proximity—
trust is a kind of proximity:
the belief of distance
keeps us safe for a time.

Still we are orbiting the sun,
which is revolving in the galaxy
around a supermassive black hole.

We are moving so fast,
leaving here too quickly to know,
but only the proximal distances
make the seasons.

Autumn:
weak sun,
strong feelings.

UTOPIAN UNDERTONES

Last night eight migrants drowned when their boat capsized
off the San Diego shoreline.

I have read about drownings in the Mediterranean,
feeling briefly sad and then angry,
always wishing Europe would change.

Is hatred like the father I saw on my walk today,
crossing the high beam of the bridge
over the dry creek-bed
one foot at a time, his young daughter following
and looking up at him—
informed by the wildflowers of fore-spring?

Inhaling deeply as I can—
now,
something I'd forgotten:

hatred reaches deeper than anger,
it brings you peace.

TEACHING PHILOSOPHY

My university will not support the prohibition
of transphobic speech
in our classrooms.

I've tried to get the language of the policy changed,
late at night facing the legalese of the faculty manual
like the hero of Kafka's "Before the Law,"
a supplicant
proposing the chiseled language of justice.

This may be because my college-bound son is trans,
but more likely because
last semester a student stopped coming to my class
after the homophobic remarks of another student—
he said two women should not raise a child.

Two decades ago or so a teacher was fired for calling his student
a Nazi—

I thought:
how could one get so emotionally wrapped up in his teaching
to make that mistake?

Did I care about my students then,
in my thirties?

It is only part of me that wants to ask for the privilege
to meet hate with contempt—

there are virtues
to being a split subject,—

irony is a language we learn
the way a native speaker learns.

GENDER STUDIES

learn
from the tire
swing—

you do it
for money,
you're good:

you do it for love,
autumn
will never
forget—

so love at last
until you're heaven
itself

REDUX

Contradictions are natural—
when someone contradicts themself
it is a sign they are alive.

But Hegel does have light to cast here:
one can grow by resolving one's contradictions—
they are not all equal,
and progress through them is possible.

Progress towards what?

The East seems to teach in its ancient texts
of Daoism and Buddhism
that presence is born of absence,
that emptiness is ultimate.

Tonight I ask them,
as a colleague once asked me when I extolled
the depth of the unconscious,—

how do you know?

NO CURE

"You're on Earth. There's no cure for that."
—Samuel Beckett

Part One

I think of Beckett's words coming home from early spring dinner
to celebrate my older son's acceptance at Berkeley,
my alma mater. Turning the corner we are confronted
with a sunset filling half the dome of the sky
with lachrymose blue and rose fire, clouds written
with splendor on the crux of mortality, beautiful and sublime,
and I feel a sense of pity for Beckett for this sentiment,
Beckett the hero of the French Resistance, son of Joyce,
who could not imagine in a credible way for himself
that Earth the curse could also be the cure.

We are out here alone on this rock: a friend said this to me,
an older friend, one with a bleak existential courage
that I have seen myself capable of but often feel is unnecessary—
there is snow on the mountain ridges
that surround this basin in which we live, the four of us,
and the blossoms of spring are here and the voices
of birds in the trees of our yard can be heard in the morning
and even, now quite often, in the middle of the night.
My wife and I bought a large world map for the wall
in my son's room when he was a young boy.
We rarely turn to it, but one of the things he is most
looking forward to in college is study abroad—
he is not sure he wants to leave home yet.

I suppose the first thing to say about the planet
is that it will not be alive forever:
nothing is more important than nothing.
There are local parables for it—the black mustard
on the hills of south county that choke out

all the natives, visitors like the coworkers
that filed in as pairs and groups to my father's hospital
room as he lay dying, strangers really,
life clinging to life and bringing death,
a vast yellow shadow that screams against the nothingness
of winter and the fate of life here,
walking on walking, as Gary Synder puts it,
the sweeping black view from the final mountain.

I audited a seminar taught by Snyder at Davis.
At one point he asked auditing students who had missed
a class session not to return. My father was passing through
for work the next week and I'd made a dinner date
with him that conflicted with the seminar.
I chose to meet with my father, and then returned to Davis
the following week. Snyder said nothing about my presence there.

So there is the matter of karma, what my teacher calls
the karmic debris, of failing an elder, transgressing—
it's a Hindu idea, filtered through the Protestant culture—
but this karmic choice also may have been
a youthful reaction against the Buddhism of Snyder,
an experience of what a book on Wallace Stevens
calls the Western scandal of nothingness, a sense that the emptiness
at the center of Snyder's Buddhist world view
was aligned with our moral catastrophes, a view strengthened
by the cold, anarchic joke he once told chuckling
about leaving the sentient world locked in a closet to suffocate.

I did learn from him something lasting
in a session where we meditated and chanted,
which led me a few months later to the Berkeley Zen Center,
where I sat zazen for months and had an experience of
meditative transcendence, the same experience I have these days
in my Daoist practice, of finding in stillness a presence
that is, as my teacher calls it, the ultimately real, though I have been left
recently with the question of what happens to the Dao
when the universe ends in a couple of trillion years—

does the Dao exist beyond this mortal cosmos?
One paradigm for play, I was reading yesterday,
is the way an infant sucks at and tongues his mother's breast
after he has fed—taking purposive behavior
and turning it to another purpose, or perhaps none at all—
perhaps this is where we learn to play,
by finding ourselves exhausting an instinct—
the mockingbird in the coast oak today
on the hillside of pear cactuses, imitating the songs
of the cactus wren and the raven and the hummingbird
for no reason that must be explained by the need to feed or to mate—
the pure joy of being alive, hearing the music of the earth
and making something of it younger than hunger.

Part Two

My older son is scared of leaving for college—
my younger son, four years his junior,
desperately wants him not to move out,
to stay and attend the local college where I teach.
We took a walk in San Juan Capistrano this Sunday afternoon
with a naturalist to see the spring wildflowers
after a winter of two months of intermittent rain—
the sweet peas and lupine made gentle statements of color
against the background of mustard and orange poppies
and grasses gone to seed—
and the scent of sage and wild anise were
surprisingly gentle too, gentle and very fresh—
the birdsong and cricket-notes mapped the hillside
the trail was cut along, and all the while,
for well over an hour, my son was quiet, perhaps sullen,
slightly scared, I knew, of mountain lion tracks,
a little lost in a region he used to call his home.

My older son has not forgotten my shrug
after he screamed in fright during a camping trip,
having found a spider in the tent he shared with his brother.

He tore through the opening of my tent in his panic
and I was furious at him for that.
Go back to sleep, I told him.
What if it's a poisonous spider? he asked.
How do you know it's not a poisonous spider?
And I shrugged. He teases me about it, a decade later.

Both of my children are directly related
to Thomas More on their mother's side,
and though they haven't read *Utopia* yet
I wonder if that fact will help them someday feel a sense
of belonging here that even our walks
and camping trips in the splendid natural scenes
of California can't or haven't—
yesterday's red tailed hawk circling and hovering
far above us, a figure for the writer in any century,
in her own element, tethered by her vision to the earth.

SUMMER HAIKU

May 7

Unopened wine-bottles
     set out for the reception—
Sunday, early evening

May midnight—
     the bird is still singing:—
his theme must be love

May 8

Monday after my fiftieth birthday—
     a late morning walk
to work on this poem—

Those loud house finches—
     the rite of youth:
song with no fear—

TOO BAD

My friend and former colleague from Duesseldorf
was visiting ten years ago, and we were talking about
my oldest child's discovery of her own nipples
years after she had been fascinated as an infant by her mother's.
"Oops," she said, laughing, in the false voice of a child—
"I have one of those, too!"

It seemed innocent at the time, innocent but deep,
and now I realize that the shock of recognition
she understood so well and playfully longed to share
with her American friends was about the Holocaust, the Shoah.

Innocence is a bane. We long for it,
politicians and gurus promise it to us—
Our love for our own innocence makes us slow
to accept the moral nuances of our lives—

We need a language of moral failure—guilt, culpability,
implication, liability, even perhaps damnation,
words that can describe our predicament somewhat accurately:
there are those who killed the indigenous people of California
in the nineteenth century, and those who encouraged
and rewarded them, and those who excused them,
and those who simply lived in the world they massacred into being.
All of us here are implicated in that bloody origin
of this most recent empire: it was a genocide that made it so,
the peaceful land over which I walk for labor and for pleasure both.

What is the cash value of this acknowledgment?
Legislators everywhere are trying to criminalize moral reflection
on our history. They know the cash value of innocence.
I think of the children of Nazis, the grandchildren of Nazis,
the pope who was in the Hitler youth—
when and how does innocence end for southern California?

The settler culture on display at Anaheim stadium,
the spontaneous roar when Ohtani hits a deep fly ball,
thousands of voices, not in concert but in agreement,
the game you win or lose before you just start again
the next day, played here all summer, the season when school is out,
when teachers do the lonely work of thinking.

RED-TAILED HAWK

Walking in Santiago Oaks with my sons and their mother
on a Sunday afternoon in May.

I tell them whoever spots the most vertebrates
can decide what I will make for dinner.

After a spell peering into the thickets
of mustard along the path,

my younger son spots a raven and then a hawk
in a swirling fight a hundred yards above us.

Then another raven appears, darting at the hawk, too.

Why are they doing that? he asks.

Probably to protect their young from the hawk, to scare him off,
I offer.

We watch them for about five minutes in silence,
separating and colliding in their tense dance.

He is rapt,
he is learning what to do when I am gone.

DOCUMENTARY

In a film about the mountains made by four men and a woman
who went together in search of unnamed canyons,

there is an opening image of fog crawling swiftly up a slope
toward the crest of a green ridge—

A poetry therapist I respect,
a Buddhist,
says she hates most poems about poetry.

That's one of the things the image of climbing mist in the mountains
makes me think of:
a world without poetry,

where every word has become heavy with mist
and the only safe passage
is on the path of doctrine.

IDEOLOGY IN LOS ANGELES

1

The first thought is about how every teacher has one thing to teach
and mine is ideology,
the idea that every material regime—
our post-industrial capitalism—
casts up like a bubbling spring a culture that naturalizes it,
falling back and soaking it all in itself.

I don't think I teach this very well—
many students get bored before the idea is clear to them.

Maybe I could begin with another example I intuit:
living in Ciudad del Carmen, Campeche, Mexico,
teaching English all summer,
going on my afternoon run for the first time in my barrio
with my headphones on
and not understanding the perplexed looks
from the residents of my neighborhood
until I happened to look behind me to check the traffic
and saw six stray dogs in a broken column
chasing me and barking up at me,

the white guy, the new guy:
for some reason you just don't run in the street around here.

2

So I got the message and began taking taxi rides
to the university track
and listening to house and techno
playing on one of three or four radio stations on the island.

I learned:
a different ideal of the public.

They were not comfortable exiles,
the German Jewish academics fleeing the Nazis,
clannish in Los Angeles,
unable or unwilling to understand the uncomplicated,
pretentious materialism of their new home
and its production of a culture profoundly suspicious of irony
and therefore imbued everywhere with its shadow,
insincerity,
which I personally think is a lousy deal for any city anywhere.

3

There is folk art in Los Angeles—
the Watts Towers of Simon Rodia,

the Great Wall of Los Angeles
of Judith Baca.

The music of Charles Mingus—
does that count?

The Getty and the Los Angeles County Museum of Art
have family art-making rooms,
rooms for children too young to care
about the museum art of others
and so who can learn the other way to discover ideology,

making art innocently themselves.

Now my children are mostly grown—
one graduating from high school, one starting it in the fall—
and I wanted to take them this summer to Watts and the valley
to see the folk art of Los Angeles,
because I knew I would be working on this poem.

But now I am a ways into it, past its beginning,
and suddenly I don't want to impose on them—

let them watch movies together for a few more weeks,
innocent in the gloom of June,

keep them for a little while longer from the critical cloud
of a parent who loved Adorno enough
to learn to read him in the original.

4

My teacher says good art often has a doubleness to it,
what Marianne Moore called gusto—

I think of that falling asleep tonight
as I recollect the first time I saw Chris Burden's *Metropolis II*
which is a huge cube of miniature roads for Hot Wheels
bustling with mechanical life
that can only be both a satire of the car-chaos of LA
and an homage to its energy—

and so it is a paradigmatic work of a city Adorno
didn't understand,

because he couldn't understand American art:
symptom and screen at once,
a vine on capitalism that cannot be autonomous
in the way of Beckett or Beethoven—

this city that cannot imagine itself without capital,
that watches its dystopian sun
set in an atmosphere that glorifies it like breath—

perhaps capital is just like breath here—
possible to control, yes—
impossible to refuse altogether.

A TRANSLATION OF RUBÉN DARÍO'S
"YO PERSIGO UNA FORMA," 1900

I'm chasing a form which my voice cannot find,
bud of thought seeking to become the rose;
it comes like a kiss my lips give shape to
at the Venus de Milo's impossible embrace.

Green palms adorn the white corridor;
the stars have predicted a vision of the goddess;
and in my soul the light reposes
like the bird of the moon resting on a tranquil lake.

I find only the words that flee,
the melodic beginning that escapes from the flute,
and the raft of dreams that drifts in space;

and beneath the window of my sleeping beauty
the unending whispers and sighs of the fountain—
the arching neck of the swan still tests me.

MORE

"Like Samuel Gompers, they want more . . . "

—Robert Hass, "Bookbuying in the Tenderloin"

THE EMBRACE OF CHAOS

—for Cornel West

1

Rage for order—
I know it well,
swing for the lost.

2

Today at the natural history museum,
looking at photos of distant nebulae:

chaos can save you, now—
free jazz
in desert weather.

3

A thought while meditating tonight
on vacation,
as my kids were at the pool
and my wife watched her show:

who could once
have been
the worst human?—

a silence
is telling me something.

4

I taught a classmate to pronounce the word,
chaos,
in eighth grade—

she is now a nurse
and a nurses union rep:

I reached in the dark

her love
for the people,

still a cold
bedfellow.

5

Like an end to suffering:

other minds,
the human rights of their bodies,

the human
wrongs and indifferences,—

late at night
their noise
made allusion to heaven.

MY HUMAN RIGHTS

as a madman
on the dock
in the rain—

something survives
of the rack
time has forgotten—

I wonder how
it survives;

no one to ask:
that's the gist
of history—

the tortured witches
and infidels,
cousins to the mad—

their discourse
is hushed,
a choice word—

between the advent
of speech

and the first day
of school:—

we all listened then,

some of us
had cried
& cried alone—

A GOOD SUMMER: THE NOTEBOOK

Gramsci and Lukacs have a more hopeful Marxist disposition than the Adorno I so adore.

I think this is in part because those two have a delicate but fierce attachment to an analytic system that Adorno has thought through to a darker skepticism.

The working class, the entrepreneur, the intellectual: firm distinctions for Gramsci and Lukacs. They trust their system completely. A child working on a proof.

I am afraid Adorno has only his education to fall back on.

I have benefited from the ethnographic argument of Jennifer Silva's *Coming Up Short*: working-class young people oppress themselves with therapeutic ideas about how they should inwardly overcome society's ways of failing them.

She calls it the mood economy. She only interviews Americans, unfortunately, but there's nothing to be done about that.

Career and marriage. Wealth. The Freudian values. What would be the values of a working-class psychoanalysis?

PSYCHOANALYSIS FROM BELOW

1

Psychoanalysis saved me.

Dr. Michael Zimmerman was his name,
in a garret office in the gourmet ghetto in Berkeley.

Sometimes I long to hear his voice again—
throaty, dramatic at moments, deeply softened by age.

But it is utterly bourgeois, right?

I am trying to imagine psychoanalysis from below,
asking a Marxist on Twitter about
how to feel the fantasy of the moment when we
"seize the forces of production,"

and on my way to the library to get a translation of *Oedipus*
late Friday night
as my headlights sweep the faculty parking lot
it occurs to me that our whole culture,
even and maybe especially the working class,
is pretty thoroughly Freudian—

self-conscious sexuality is everywhere,
hostility and aggression are insincerely veiled,

we all feel we need to adapt ourselves
in the searchlight of an empire.

2

Rereading *Oedipus* from the perspective
of a working class psychoanalysis
the first thought that occurs to me
is that Tiresias is a pretty good allegory for the intellectual
in our society—

coerced to tell the truth,
and then disbelieved.

But the working class is, allowing for differences,
in the play too—

the whole set up of the work is that the masses in Thebes
are suffering terribly,
and they look to their patrician lord to help them—

then the play takes the swerve
that the literature of the canon of my youth took too,
away from the interests of the people,
to the drama and depth of the lives of the privileged few.

So I suppose the Oedipus complex
of the working class
is to understand that self-interest and self-involvement
are the golden rule of culture,
that the subtleties of the mind and the human heart
work like a car chase on our culture.

3

Another insight the Marxists had first, there—
that was the point of socialist realism.

I suppose you could say of Freud in the thirties
when he turned to social questions
that he was too much of a realist for socialist realism.

So what would be a Freudian socialist realism?

Impossible to imagine.
But I suppose in the same way
it is impossible to imagine a working class academy,
or a working class Christianity—

the only power for the worker
is the very real power
of having no skin in the game,

the immense fury and resentment and force
of Clare Daly in the European Parliament,

the great luxury I long for
even as working class resentment embarrasses me—

the moral wealth of not being a hypocrite.

4

That said,
there are many working class whites who hate socialism.

I read a book about the antisemitism of philosophy
and it argued persuasively that German culture
is turned by the Greeks against the Jews—

just as the Mexican poets troped towards the French
or the Americans towards the English,

there is something biased in German philosophy towards
the opposite of the Jews.

In that sense,
Freud is a blind theorist of the abject.

He asked, What does woman want?
He was not sure of his answer.

The same could be said
of the desire of the working class in his thinking—
no answer there.

More, said Samuel Gompers.

Having taken a walk to think about it, I have another hypothesis—
not so much more as better,
better art especially,

and time,
time in relation to their art.

ORTEGA HIGHWAY

The one road traversing
the Santa Ana mountains from west to east
begins twenty-five miles south of my home,

in San Juan Capistrano,
a paved highway
on the track cut by the coastal indigenous tribe,
the Acjachemen,

over millennia of trading with the desert tribes
on the other side of the mountains.

Another poet described rush-hour
as a groove cut
by the magnet of love and the magnet of work.

The magnet of trade—
can one speak this way?

What carried them through the mountains like—

a plume of ash?
a pod on a gust of wind?

They were innocent of Hannah Arendt's distinction
between labor and work:

work survives,
labor leaves no trace.

ESSAY ON MOTOWN

1

"There is no lost feast at the bottom of memory—invent!"

These were the words of my teacher
to fifteen younger poets at the end of the twentieth century,
meeting in a long narrow room with threadbare sofas
beneath a bank of windows that looked out
onto Doe Library,
gathering twice a week over a beautiful Berkeley spring.

Today I was talking about Diego Rivera at dinner
with my children and my wife,
and I felt overwhelmed by a memory
that must be, at least in part, an invention:

as an eight-year-old, taken to the Detroit Institute of Art
with my mother and sister and a family friend, David,
and his three young children—

feeling mistreated, transparently asked to feign interest
in works that filled me with boredom,
works that I could make no sense of,
that seemed pointless like the overheard conversations
of adults everywhere,
resentful, even at that young age, of my powerlessness,

and then arriving in the room with the Diego Rivera murals
celebrating the industrial working class,
the sweepingly powerful forms of the workers on assembly lines,
and knowing that something special had just happened to me,
that I had felt what it means to invent
and so felt how artfully one could love
the culture and people of my ugly hometown of Detroit.

2

The Bleacher Creatures.
That's what they called the fans who sat in the backless cheap seats
of Tiger Stadium,
shirtless, long-haired, younger than my father.

One memory of what I learned from them about manhood
was the game I went to around age ten,
sitting adjacent to the bleachers, close enough to see
a man who had captured a moth
that had been battering around an exposed lightbulb—
he held it in an empty beer cup
and the crowd cheered him on, chanting at him to do it,
and after a long time mugging, he grabbed the moth by its wings
and washed it down his throat with a gulp of his friend's beer.

The bleachers erupted in cheers for him.

I wondered at these men who were so different from my father,
their coarseness,—

they scared me,
how easily they could be distracted by themselves
and their hairy, self-celebrating bodies
from what we were all there for,
the men who played a game.

3

Motown music and Motown Records
were born about eight years before I was—
an important interval.

Every new generation of pop music seems
to rediscover transgression
of sexually repressive customs,
to exult in the new emergence of sexuality
like the subtle force of the blossoming pear tree in spring.

Motown was the first to celebrate in a way the culture was ready for
this sexual energy of black musicians,
and long before I knew anything consciously
about slavery or Jim Crow or the Great Migration
I watched a young girl dance in the street
in a bikini while the fire hydrant was opened to gush cool water
to mitigate the heat of summer,—

my girl—my guy:
music I came late to,

long before I knew about the Riots of 1967,
I knew about the survival of sexuality
and the blossoming that cares nothing about the fruit.

BARBENHEIMER SUMMER

1

Two hours into the movie,
after the dropping of the bombs on Hiroshima and Nagasaki,
Oppenheimer pivots to a sub-plot
about the disgrace of the hero years after the event.
We saw the film last night as a family, the four of us.
What did you think?, my older son asked.
It went on too long, I told him.
He was almost trembling—
I have never had a cinematic experience this intense, he said.
He seemed a little disappointed,
perhaps even hurt, by my opinion.

Later, discussing it in a candlelit living room at midnight,
I told him this, learning as I spoke:
there's nothing about the Japanese victims, I said.
The images of white coworkers dying that haunts Oppenheimer
is about his own inner world,
not about the great moral question, the moral theme,
involved in the film.

I know it's not that kind of a movie, I said.
It's a Hollywood blockbuster.
But that's why I said it went on too long.
I couldn't care about the embarrassment of a few
scientists when the great problem of representing
the suffering of a hundred thousand innocents
goes unaddressed, ignored,
even in a way stigmatized.

It made me feel sad, I said.
And then it made me feel lonely.

2

I wonder about the ways history shapes the present—
the limit of negative capability,
to be in uncertainty without grasping at truth and fact,—
it's tested by this mystery.

Teleology—
the great theistic answer to the question:
the goodness of the present
explains the sadness of the past.

It becomes the great academic answer:
one chapter, thirty pages, per period of history.

And I suppose at root that is as Puritan as any answer, too:
the end of history is a book about history.

3

When I meditate these days
I hear myself screaming as an infant,
hospitalized and subjected to a spinal tap,
alone, without the comfort of a mother's touch.

That scream is the scream of history;
there has been a human being screaming
for the last two thousand years.

Abreaction:
the purging of a trauma by talking about it.

It works for some individuals, sometimes.
It probably never works for societies.

So do the traumatized relate to history differently?

My Daoist teacher likes the story of the teacher who says
to his disciple:
how many people you brought here with you!

What do you mean? It's just me—says the disciple.

Precisely so, answers the teacher.

4

In my moment:

The ignorant in Florida prohibit teaching
the disgrace of slavery.

One of the traumas I confront in writing for the people
is the death of Vincent Chin
at the hands of two unemployed autoworkers outside of a bar
in Detroit when I lived there at nine years old.

I take this today as proof that traumatic moral injury
to the United States cannot be abreacted,
by the body politic or by me.

Why do we need to talk about the past then,
if there is no reason to expect healing?

To allow suffering to speak,
the answer of Cornel West and Czeslaw Milosz.
But why—on what grounds?

My children just came in the room to talk about baseball
as I was trying to finish this line of thought—

and I talked with them,
laughing,
almost grateful to be interrupted and feel less alone
with the masses.

MENSCH

This is what my seminar teacher
called Raymond Williams
because he taught at working class schools—

the white savior complex,—
what makes it complicated?

Another experience of the word:
when I taught American Studies in Germany
and at an exam the department head called a student to his face
ein fleissiger Mensch,

a hardworking guy.

Etymologies can be helpful—
the word goes back to Guy Fawkes Day,
celebrating a terrorist.

But: a great guy,
that's how we express the word *Mensch*—

the forgiveness of history
like a lost accent,—

what would you teach at a working class school?
What Chomsky nostalgically calls high culture,
celebrating the aspirations
of nineteenth century industrial workers?

The novel?
The plays of Shakespeare,

the concept of art
as an uncommitted crime?

SEXUAL PERSONAE

I wear my tie askew—
                    that says I'm always working,
          but not for you—

WHITE EXPECTATIONS

The conversation about whiteness when I was in my twenties sought to see it through the eyes of its others, its victims.

The purpose of studying whiteness was to dismantle white supremacism. That is my hope too.

But maybe we are going about it wrong—what if the path beyond white supremacism is not away from, but towards whiteness: to get so close that the concept disintegrates.

One semester an African student, Belinda, posed a question, not so much to me as through me.

It's not hard for me to understand how white people could do this, she said, speaking of chattel slavery. I just don't understand their need to justify themselves.

I said nothing and have not broken that silence yet.

I think my answer is that humans are complicated beings.

THE DECLINE AND FALL OF THE MAYA EMPIRE

I believe the anthropologists
who say that since the dawn of agriculture
ten thousand years ago
there has always been a ruling class.

So: taxes, standing armies, gender roles—
the whole modern shebang.

The question is:
how to understand the people who inhabit these roles,—

are they the weeds I saw a gardener poisoning in a rock-bed
this morning on my walk to work?—

priests,
holding aloft a human heart?

I think tradition creates the structure of caste;
and then, in every culture,
scared mortals,
not essentially different from you and me,
though, perhaps,
slightly less decided about their human nature,
rush up the mountain of status like trees to the timberline.

So that's the metaphor:
the timberline,

past which a hermit can of course rise,
one willing to learn about the invention of the white race:

to read its terrifyingly complete history,
and so perhaps to lose his nature for a time,
to transplant his body with his shadow.

HAIKU WRITTEN WHILE READING
THE INVENTION OF THE WHITE RACE

The oak at night—
not quite
the oak at sunset—

FOR ROBERT

The first strong wind of autumn
and the old men are bent
in the afternoon on campus
gathering the fallen leaves
into a bundle wrapped by a white tarp.

They fold up the tarp
and tie the ends together
and move the bundles
to the back of pickup trucks—

they seem to keep their eyes on their work,
not to admire it, I believe,
but to avoid the feelings that might be provoked
by sustained eye contact with those walking by.

Is earth the right place for love?
Sometimes.
The extremes of summer, the extremes of winter:

every day has its firsts,—
today's first was an extreme
in the river of autumn,—

silent as a man
who argues with himself.

BERKELEY PREQUEL

The ant of fear,
the ash.

Rising in the window,
the joy of mortality.

And then after,
life sweetens.

You know the rain,
the tonic tribe,

the fruit
fit for vision.

Between us
the third death
comes like a shadow.

To turn the corner
of forever.

Keep quiet
in class

about everything
but them.

Who they are—
they could do great things

that won't save
a seated soul.

Suffering
has its form,—

if I should die
before I wake

I pray the Lord
to play,

here and there,
so quietly.

Emily would
not look away:

what would she see
in that child?

No one is watching
the sun

from every angle,
the senses

of chemistry
are in autumn,

the sense
of where you look

when you
look away

is its emptiness
destroyed—

LOSER ODE

1

When I was young and then when my children were young
my mother would buy an extra hamburger
at the drive-thru if she'd seen
a homeless person,
and she would give them the food
without much comment to me or to my kids.

It seemed natural to me for a time as a child,
then for years it seemed grotesque—why?—
and now again it seems admirable,
as I leave my literary theory course on today's topic of disability
and so many of my students—at least four—
have said the coldest things about people
with invisible disabilities.

To be defeated:
if you are, everyone distrusts you in America—
almost everyone,
but not me, so much, anymore—
I've had a midlife thawing of the heart.

2

The fear not so much of losing
but of being a loser:

I think that explains the appeal of Trump
and the racism James Baldwin dissected—
to be passionate for a rich white hater
means one hasn't yet lost the game of American life.

I do wonder about my Trumpist aunt
who has boundless compassion for homeless veterans.
Compassion begins at home, she says.

It's taken a certain coldness for me myself to get this far.

I remember when I was depressed in college
sitting at the corner one Saturday night
watching couples leave the movie theater,
all of them ignoring the panhandler underneath the marquee
asking for spare change.

I think I even cried for a while after an hour beholding the sight.
But I had my own work to do, eventually—

analyzing a Shakespearean sonnet,
asking forty questions about how to teach it in my thesis,
using the phrase "theory and praxis,"

learning that charity is nothing without changing the system,
learning that the system teaches us
how to read poems well.

3

So one simply cannot feel all the compassion
called for by our human predicament.

Detachment, says Buddha, the path away from suffering.

My wife was almost the director of a nonprofit
for the kids of the families that pick through the dump
in Guatemala City.

She came back home from her final interview there in a parka
marked with bird-shit
and went straight to the shower before she spoke to us.

I envied her.

Compassion will not save you.
It will not save everyone else.

And perhaps at a certain point it becomes perverse.

But perhaps we should pause longer at compassion
before we rush to grief.

The dead only belong to some of us;
the suffering belong to us all.

LAW LIKE, LOVE LIKE

Trying to remember when I first learned the law
exists apart from your own goodness,
that you are not the sunlight
but the sundial.

There are memories,
connected like traces to the nub of the pen,—
none of them explain
why I can still believe in Law,
in whose coldness alone I could not survive,
why I believe, against evidence perhaps,
that, though it is not designed to protect the weak,
it can do so,
tonight, tomorrow—especially tonight and tomorrow.

I think of two bodies getting into bed
in a cold room in which
they could feel the tightness of their skin,
the chill at the edges of their eyes.

Slowly they warm in the bed together,
and they do not need
to trust one another,
they can feel how they bring each other protection,
simply, naturally.

Say one body is a black body
and one is white—

by the law of memory,
this could only be my wish.

UNTITLED

I remember today
in my first semester of teaching
I found it humorous
that in my student evaluations
one student simply said:
you use the word resist too much.

I had then many classmates
with more of what our professors called
political sophistication,
one of whom taught Palestinian literature
in a composition course
and ignited a controversy.

Now my child is studying
at that same school,
sending me pictures from the stately
study room of the library
in the early evening,
his tablet open before him.

Do you know what it means to resist?
In the anatomy of hope
something must be the blood.
In the books we read
there is always a rebirth:
the past born from the body of the past.

PRAYER

I attended a vigil tonight
just to mourn—

for I have for decades looked past
the targets of my rage—

to the distant future—

I learned tonight:

one hundred years, or so,
at most,
that's as far as a human heart can care—

candles,
the code of the candles

as they lit them,
the Muslims and Christians and Jews,
and me, the Daoist,—

its ordinary beauty at nightfall,—

THE WILLOW

William Butler Yeats said it first:
we make poems out of our arguments with ourselves.

One that began for me was when I saw in an interview
on the carpet before an awards event
Jim Carrey say with depth and playfulness,
circling his hand in the gesture of a physical comedian—

none of this matters.

He meant everything that happens on our small planet.
I thought first:
how sad for you not to know love.

And subsequently I have thought:
how well you might love, given this darkness.

Looking downward,
crossing a shallow stream today with my family,
I don't know when I noticed the pollen drifting

right at us, at eye level,
tufted into the air from a willow above.

It came into my awareness
like a voice on waking slowly
from sleep in mid-morning.

It mattered for a moment
because it seemed snatched from uselessness
by consciousness, pure consciousness,

a caution to listen to
the message of beauty,
a message which belongs to neither heaven nor earth.

FOR MELANIE

You ask if I believe
we will still be together
after we die.

I think of my student who answered my own question about a poem
by saying,
I believe something can be two things at once.

The yucca sends up its stalk
in autumn,
in the neighbors' yard,—

dance as protest,
that is where I first found you,
a protest against sadness—

In dying we become something new,—
who finds out what we become?

In this life we have already been together
after death,—

this has always been our pact:
with each new sadness,
a dance.

PERSPECTIVE

I would like to keep things in perspective,
as the text on resilience says I should.

I could go for a walk at Santiago Oaks—
it drizzled all day today,
so the path will be muddy and slippery tomorrow morning.

So maybe I can contemplate something else beautiful—
a work of art.

Paintings sometimes remind me of my smallness;
Rembrandt's genius does this,
and abstract expressionism.

When I was despairing in my daughter's infancy,
I feared the ocean;

I would drive to it all the way through the canyon
and turn away at the very end.

Today I heard it and smelled it from very close—
it is so different that way from the idea of it,

everything it has to say:
it's there always

BRIAN GLASER is the author of six books of poetry and many essays on poetry and poetics. He lives in Santa Ana, California, and teaches art and history at Chapman University.

• sites.chapman.edu/bglaser

SHANTI ARTS

NATURE • ART • SPIRIT

Please visit us online
to browse our entire book catalog,
including poetry collections and fiction,
books on travel, nature, healing, art,
photography, and more.

Also take a look at our highly regarded art
and literary journal, *Still Point Arts Quarterly*,
which may be downloaded for free.

www.shantiarts.com

www.ingramcontent.com/pod-product-compliance
Lightning Source LLC
Chambersburg PA
CBHW022039090426
42741CB00007B/1132